Just a Girl Who Loves Gymnastics Series

This Journal Belongs To

Made in United States
Troutdale, OR
12/05/2024

25944119R00071